NORTHAMPTON
WELCOME TO THE PAST

PART ONE

Highways and Byways

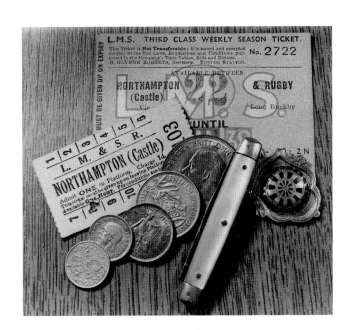

Frontispiece. In an almost Dickensian scene, children play their timeless games around the paved Victorian cul-de-sac of St James's Square, watched over by a solitary gas lamp. Not to be confused with the town's St James area, St James Square was situated off St James's Street, the building at the rear backing onto properties in Woolmonger Street. Old as this picture may seem, it was taken on Thursday 2 August 1962. *(Northampton Chronicle & Echo)*

NORTHAMPTON
WELCOME TO THE PAST

PART ONE

Highways and Byways

by

RICHARD COLEMAN and JOE RAJCZONEK

W.D. WHARTON

Wellingborough

First published in 1994
Reprinted 1996

W.D. Wharton
37 Sheep Street
Wellingborough
Northamptonshire NN8 1BX

Text copyright © Richard Coleman and Joe Rajczonek 1994

Richard Coleman and Joe Rajczonek assert their moral right
to be identified as the authors of this work

ISBN 0 9518557 7 8

Designed and typeset by John Hardaker, Wollaston, Northamptonshire
Printed and bound in Great Britain by
Butler & Tanner Ltd
Frome, Somerset

ACKNOWLEDGEMENTS

Our sincere thanks are extended to the following people and organizations. The unnamed photographers of both the *Northampton Chronicle & Echo* and Northampton Borough Council.

The named photographers who have generously allowed us the use of their material, including John Meredith for the use of his father's negatives. We also acknowledge that some of the earlier images may well have originated from Henry Cooper, a well-known local photographer around the turn of the century.

Judith Hodgkinson, for helping track down some of the photographic items.

Northampton Mercury Co., in particular Robin Fletcher the Editor, who not only gave us permission to use the *Chronicle & Echo* negative collection but also very kindly wrote the foreword to this book.

Northampton Borough Council, especially Bridget Peet and Sinead Walsh for the use of the Borough negatives from both the Council's own photographers and the archive collection.

Northamptonshire Libraries, for giving us free access to the *Chronicle & Echo* negative collection.

Jess Lay, for his retouching skills.

Special thanks to Mark Higlett, who coped admirably with our constant pressure to provide top quality hand prints from the negatives provided for use in the book.

Finally, our many thanks to the production team – John Hardaker for his continuing patience in face of our numerous requests to alter and amend our original layout and manuscript; Mick Sanders for answering our incessant questions about printing techniques; and finally Robert Wharton who has given us great freedom in the preparation of the book.

Half title caption
Pocket contents. *(Richard Coleman)*

Title page caption
The fog hangs thick in the air in the vicinity of the Racecourse on Kettering Road during the night of Thursday 30 October 1958. As the cars crawl past, a lady patiently waits for her bus opposite the Picturedrome cinema.
(Northampton Chronicle and Echo)

Front end-paper captions
(Left) The maker's drawing of the Market Square fountain in its original form.
(Northampton Borough Council Archive)

(Right) The architect's line and wash drawing of the Emporium Arcade.
(Northampton Borough Council Archive)

Rear end-paper captions
(Left) The print of the new Town Hall that was presented with the Northampton Mercury on 21 May 1864. *(Northampton Borough Council Archive)*

(Right) The procession notice for laying the foundation stone of the new Town Hall on 22 October 1861. *(Northampton Borough Council Archive)*

CONTENTS

FOREWORD

As a well-known landmark changes and evolves over the years it is easy to forget how things used to be. Northampton's Market Square has had its fair share of change in recent times – beginning with the removal of the old fountain and ending (for the moment) with the building of the Grosvenor Centre.

The now demolished *Chronicle & Echo* and *Mercury & Herald* offices on the corner of the Market Square were a landmark within a landmark. From the outside their incongruous form always looked both out of place and yet perfectly at home among older neighbouring buildings. From the inside the Mercury Company's team of photographers, whose spirit and skill was epitomized by the work of Roland Holloway, had a window on the world.

Their ideal vantage point gave them a unique opportunity to observe Northampton, and particularly the Market Square as it shed its old and familiar look and embraced the modern world. Fortunately this opportunity was rarely wasted, and the changes around them were faithfully recorded in glorious black and white – still today the most evocative form of photography.

Since the *Chronicle & Echo* moved to the Upper Mounts, many of the thousands of negatives produced during the period 1950 to 1970 have rested, untouched and perhaps forgotten, in Northampton Central Library. Now, thanks to the patience, skill and determination of Richard Coleman and Joe Rajczonek, originators and authors of this book, discarded ancient images are being brought back to life.

Many of today's younger generation may be bemused or curious about the widespread fascination with how Northampton used to be. But for those who were there, who still have precious images captured in their mind's eye, this book offers a free passage to the past.

We must never stand in the way of progress – but, as this book clearly demonstrates, we should never forget the past either.

Robin Fletcher
Editor
Northampton Mercury Co.

INTRODUCTION

In Northampton's well-documented history there is a tendency for the Victorian era to be used as a point of reference to measure changes that have taken place in the town. There certainly has been a transformation since the turn of the century, but the greater part of it has been compacted into just the last 30 years. Almost overnight, it seems, many well-known landmarks and even streets have disappeared, and whole areas have changed beyond recognition to make way for new roads, car parks and modern buildings.

The fact is that in our lifetime the old heart has been cut out of the town. Some two thirds of it has been rebuilt in one way or another, and fine examples of architecture and craftsmanship have been laid flat to make room for gaunt structures of concrete and glass – hardening the town's character and making it a less friendly place to be in.

Rather than just a collection of buildings and streets, the old town centre was a way of life for many people. Factories, warehouses, pubs, streets of terraced houses, places of entertainment, hotels, town houses – all used to be close together and within easy walking distance.

In this book we have tried to recall some of those scenes that have gone for ever. We have not set out to cover every single building or street that has disappeared, but to take a nostalgic look back to the not too distant past through a special selection of photographs. Some of them have appeared in the *Chronicle & Echo* over the years and although a few occasionally reappeared in different publications, most of the images have long since been forgotten.

To have put all the pictures that we selected into one book would have been an impossibility, so we decided to spread them over two volumes. This, the first volume, shows predominantly street views in the area around the town centre. The second volume will portray the people of Northampton, the special occasions in the town, the personalities who came to visit and many other nostalgic scenes.

We hope the books will appeal not just to those who are Northamptonians born and bred, but also to the many people who have moved to Northampton during the last three decades and who perhaps do not realize how much the town has changed.

Whilst compiling the book we were surprised, despite the years we have been associated with the town as home and workplace, how little we had really noticed the variety of architecture that was once there to be seen. Some still remains, and we urge you to look above the shopfronts and become more aware of it before it, too, is swept away.

For that which has already gone, this book stands as a memorial, and we welcome you to Northampton's past.

Richard Coleman and Joe Rajczonek

Market Square Memories

1. The scaffolding erected for the remedial works to All Saints Church tower provides a grandstand view of the Market Square's north side on Tuesday 22 July 1958. The first markets were held on this site in the year 1235 during the reign of Henry III. *(Northampton Chronicle & Echo)*

2. Northampton Market Square on a typical Saturday during March 1953, and the square is packed with people doing their weekend shopping. At the top of the fountain, the 'crows nest' and four hanging lamps appear quite elegant, especially from this angle. *(Northampton Chronicle & Echo)*

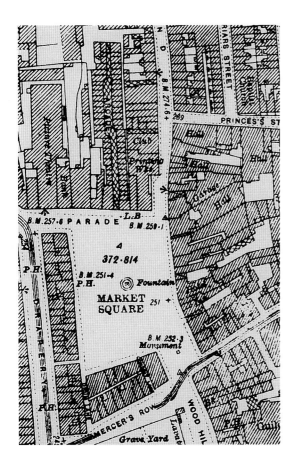

3. This pre-war 1939 photograph of Market Square was taken from the top of the new *Chronicle & Echo* building which had reached roof level, and the line of the brickwork can just be seen at the bottom of the picture. The array of vehicles below, both parked and moving, is enough to quicken the pulse of today's classic car enthusiasts.
(Northampton Chronicle & Echo)

4. Almost 20 years later than the previous picture, and in very different weather conditions on Tuesday 25 February 1958, the scene from the same viewpoint has changed very little, though keen-eyed observers will spot the modification to the top of the fountain. The way the snow has attractively picked out the detail on the buildings, in particular the fountain and All Saints Church tower, was probably not appreciated at the time by the few pedestrians about, their coat collars turned up against the biting winter wind. One can almost feel the extreme cold coming off the page! *(Northampton Chronicle & Echo)*

5. Over the years many words, both complimentary and derogatory, have been written about the Market Square fountain, donated to the town by Captain Samuel Isaacs in 1863 and made by Messrs Barwell and Co. No doubt it will have looked at its best in its original form (see front end-paper) painted dark blue with detail picked out in gold, but before the turn of the century a far less impressive lamp was fitted, and this remained until October 1930 when refurbishments included a set of four new electric 'snowdrop' lamps, the construction of the 'crows nest' (see picture 2) and a repaint in green and gold. Thereafter the feature's appearance gradually deteriorated and it ended up being painted an unattractive utility green. The lamps were removed in 1953, followed by the 'crows nest' in 1954 to be replaced by a copper sphere and four modern light fittings insensitively bolted under the column's top-plate. Years of neglect eventually led to the fountain's removal on 15 April 1962 – less than a week after this photograph was taken.
(Northampton Borough Council)

6. The copper sphere, made and donated by Airflow Streamlines Ltd, of Main Road, Far Cotton, is installed at the top of the fountain's column on Monday 30 August 1954. When the fountain was removed in 1962 the sphere was returned to Airflow. *(Northampton Chronicle & Echo)*

7. (facing page) The Peacock Hotel photographed from the *Chronicle & Echo* building on Saturday 2 May 1959. Six months later it was demolished. What were the town planners thinking about? A hotel or inn had stood on this site for nearly 500 years. The building seen here was built in different stages, starting in 1676 after the great fire had burnt down its predecessor, and at one time it was a well-known coaching inn with stabling for over 30 horses. The Peacock Hotel had its own particular character and old world charm. *(Northampton Chronicle & Echo)*

8. (right) The balcony of The Peacock was often used by politicians and others for addressing people below in the Market Square. In this unique view we look out from the first floor meeting room over the balcony to the fountain on Monday 4 May 1959. *(Northampton Chronicle & Echo)*

...hrough the main entrance of The Peacock from Market ...otographed during the summer of 1936 and shows the first ... area. Through the next bridge the start of the second inner ... be seen. This is where the stabling for the horses and accommodation for the coachmen and grooms used to be. At this time the inn was called The Peacock Commercial and Midland Railway Hotel, hence the railway timetable notice boards on either side of the entrance. *(W.J.S. Meredith)*

10. Another view of the courtyard at The Peacock, photographed from near the Assembly Room door, seen in the previous picture, on Monday 4 May 1959 looking out through the main entrance on to Market Square. By this time pillars had been positioned under the timber beam to support the first floor structure. *(Northampton Chronicle & Echo)*

11. A beautiful stained glass panel from within The Peacock Hotel. One can imagine its subtle colours, especially when lit from behind. Surely it must still be in existence somewhere? This photograph was taken on Monday 4 May 1959. *(Northampton Chronicle & Echo)*

12. Buses queue up on the Market Square outside the Northampton Corporation offices in preparation for a Holiday Tour during the Easter weekend at the beginning of April 1956. Local tours were a popular feature during the 1950s, and Northampton Corporation Transport Company were obviously expecting a good turnout with ten double-deckers already in view – but where are all the passengers? *(Northampton Chronicle & Echo)*

13. A typical Saturday scene on 30 July 1966 photographed from the bottom of the Market that has altered little over the years. The buildings in view around the perimeter of the square, however, have all gone. At the bottom of Newland, the building with lettering on the roof slates is Welsh House in its final form prior to demolition during 1973.
(Northampton Chronicle & Echo)

14. A time exposure captures this nocturnal view from a window in the *Chronicle & Echo* building, while down below the stall holders appear to be doing some brisk business as shoppers crowd the Market Square on Saturday 19 December 1953, the last Saturday shopping before Christmas. *(Northampton Chronicle & Echo)*

15. Following the previous night's snow, the sun makes a welcome appearance as council workmen clear pathways around the stalls to make shopping a little less hazardous for those prepared to brave the elements on Thursday 5 March 1970. *(Northampton Chronicle & Echo)*

16. Drama at the Market Square on Saturday 24 April 1965 as stalls catch fire (also setting light to the adjacent van), the flames quickly spreading in the gusty wind. Fortunately, the Fire Brigade soon arrived on the scene to bring matters under control, although the lad is doing the best he can to stop the fire spreading by stamping out the burning debris with his winkle-picker shoes. (*Northampton Chronicle & Echo*)

17. and 18. For a time during 1959 UFOs, and particularly flying saucers, were in the news, so the *Chronicle & Echo* photographers decided to conjure up a picture for the evening paper. The end-result on Saturday 30 May 1959 shows three lady shoppers gazing skywards as a flying saucer hovers in the sky on the other side of All Saints church – at least, that's the *Chronicle & Echo's* story. *(Northampton Chronicle & Echo)*

19. Following the move from the old kiosk on Wood Hill, A.G. Eckford's brand new mobile kiosk stands at the bottom of Market Square on Friday 1 January 1954. The new kiosk, of polished hardwood with aluminium trims, was very smart and roomy, and was made locally for the bargain price of £600. As usual, the kiosk was being run by Mrs A.G. Eckford, daughter D.M. Ward and sister-in-law Mrs M. Eckford (see pictures 53 and 54). *(Northampton Chronicle & Echo)*

20. Wednesday 30 December 1953, and 'Darkie', the last parcels delivery horse at Northampton, plods along the wet cobbles of The Parade at the top of Market Square. Aboard is carter Tom Tilley and they are on their final round, bringing to an end the use of horse-drawn parcels vans after 80 years service. This day's round started from Castle Station at 8 a.m., and on return 'Darkie' would be put on a train and sent to London to face a very uncertain future. The nine goods horses that remained in railway service at Northampton were far more fortunate, as a fund was set up by some local people and they were bought from British Railways as they were withdrawn during 1954. *(Northampton Chronicle & Echo)*

21. One horse power against many was bound to lose out in the march of progress, but it was very pleasing to see the environmentally friendly horse still making an appearance on the Market Square as late as 1959 – Tuesday 14 April to be exact. *(Northampton Chronicle & Echo)*

22. As the new *Chronicle & Echo* building progresses in 1939, the inevitability of World War II could be sensed by the urgency to recruit 1500 Territorials in Northamptonshire. The building's new exterior, in contrast to the cars parked nearby, seems to suggest that architectural design was ahead of motor car styling. *(Northampton Chronicle & Echo)*

23. During the latter part of World War II a Royal Air Force display toured the country as part of a drive to raise money for the war effort by encouraging people to buy National Savings War Bonds, Certificates or Stamps. 'Wings for Victory' week at Northampton was from 7-15 May 1943, and for the occasion a Lancaster bomber (F for Freddie), a Tiger Moth and a Spitfire were put on show in the Market Square. There was also an exhibition in the Town Hall. The target for the Northampton area was £750,000 – enough to buy 15 Lancasters and 30 Spitfires, but by the end of the week the target had been exceeded by nearly 50 per cent (sufficient for 22 Lancasters and 45 Spitfires). In this picture the Spitfire is being set up on the Square.
(Northampton Borough Council Archive – Cyril Arnold)

24. The Market Square was often used as a collection and refreshment point for the Services and other organizations involved in civic duties – in this case for the visit of HM Queen Elizabeth II to the town on Friday 9 September 1965. *(Northampton Chronicle & Echo)*

25. One of the annual events on the Market was the 'Lorry Driver of the Year' contest, seen here on Tuesday 31 July 1962 with a lorry driver giving his vehicle a final polish as the judges carry out inspections and take notes.

In the centre of the market, the base and lamps are a sad reminder of the fountain's removal some three-and-a-half months earlier.
(*Northampton Chronicle & Echo*)

26. The much lamented Emporium Arcade stands proudly on the north side of Market Square on Tuesday 26 July 1966. The building was designed by Mosely and Scrivener of Northampton and was erected in 1910 by A.J. Chown, accommodating around 50 shop units, several suites of offices and a large room used as a billiards hall during the 1920s and 30s.

The main entrance was from Market Square with two side entrances off Newland. Sadly the efforts to save the building, or at least its frontage, failed, and it was demolished during the early part of 1972 to make way for a more modern characterless building. *(Northampton Chronicle & Echo)*

27. Thursday 31 December 1959, and the Emporium Arcade is up for sale. The ornate Market Square entrance facade was made from purple, green and white Doulton tiles – samples of which are stored in the Northampton Museum. *(Northampton Chronicle & Echo)*

28. Photographs taken inside the Emporium Arcade have been very difficult to find. This view, taken on a rather dull day during October 1970, is looking from the top of the arcade towards the off-centre octagonal area and the Market Square. The octagonal area was fitted with a domed glass roof.
(Peter Staughton)

29. A view along the section of arcade that led from the Market Square to the off-centre octagonal area. This section had no balconies and a differently designed roof to the rear section. By the number of people milling about, it appears the arcade was still being patronized by Northampton shoppers when this photograph was taken during October 1970. This is the same picture that appears in colour on the back of the book jacket.
(Peter Staughton)

30. Although taken as demolition was about to begin in 1972 (from nearly the same position as in picture 28) this photograph reveals the elegance of the balconied interior of the top section of the Emporium Arcade, consisting of numerous small shops with offices above. This was the view from the top of the arcade looking towards the Market Square. The car is standing in the off-centre octagonal area about half way up the arcade, off which a run of shops led to one of the side entrances in Newland (shown in picture 36). *(Northampton Borough Council)*

31. The Arcade is still well in use in this early 1960s view looking out on to a sunny Saturday market. The curved ceiling and ornate ironwork at the entrance sets the scene for the elegance within. *(L.H. Cummings)*

32. This unusual picture, photographed from inside the *Chronicle & Echo* building while under construction in 1939, gives a glimpse of the lamps and 'crows nest' at the top of the fountain, with All Saints in the background. Amazingly, despite the disruption of the major remodelling of the building's exterior, the newspaper carried on production within. *(Northampton Chronicle & Echo)*

33. A pre-1931 photograph of the *Northampton Mercury* building on the corner of Newland shows the advertising hoarding erected after road widening by the demolition of the end building circa 1910. During 1931 the two weekly papers – *Northampton Mercury* and *Northampton Herald* – were combined. Likewise, the two daily papers – *Daily Chronicle* and *Daily Echo* – were merged to form the *Chronicle & Echo*, the first issue of which appeared on 2 November 1931 – price 1d for 12 pages. *(Northampton Chronicle & Echo)*

34. An intriguing view along the scaffolding shows the small arch details of the building on the opposite page at the start of demolition works in 1938.

Note the rope-lashed wooden scaffold poles with uprights positioned in sand-filled barrels. *(Northampton Chronicle & Echo)*

35. A glimpse down Newland on a wet and dismal December day in 1938 finds work on the old *Chronicle & Echo* building under way, the exterior of which, after transformation, looked totally out of character with the rest of Market Square. The entrance on the right with its ornate metal-covered sliding doors saw frequent use with regular deliveries of large rolls of newsprint for use on the printing presses. *(Northampton Chronicle & Echo)*

36. Another wet day, and rain glistens on the road and pavements in Newland on Thursday 16 April 1964. On the corner of Princess Street the Temperance Hall Cinema has just been converted for use as a Bingo Hall.

On the left can be seen one of the two entrances to the Emporium Arcade that were situated in Newland. (*Northampton Chronicle & Echo*)

37. As the final section of wooden scaffolding is dismantled and loaded on to a waiting lorry the new exterior of the *Chronicle & Echo* building is revealed in this 1939 view.
(Northampton Chronicle & Echo)

38. During the refuse strike in 1966 some groups of people with access to a lorry set themselves up as pirate dustmen. Here we see one such group surreptitiously loading up outside Welsh House Chambers at the bottom of Newland on Tuesday 26 July 1966. Welsh House was said to be the only building on the Market to survive the great fire in 1675, but sadly it wasn't so lucky when the Grosvenor Centre was built – although an excellent replica frontage was constructed, returning the building to the way it looked during the 1830s.
(Northampton Chronicle & Echo)

39. At the bottom of Newland on the beautiful sunny morning of Saturday 20 June 1959 Mr Spencer Gunn's vintage 1912 Wolsley advertises the Blind Association garden fête at Wardington Court on the Welford Road.

Behind the car is one of the very quiet water-cooled LE Velocette motor cycles, commonly referred to as 'Noddy bikes' owing to their use by the police force. *(Northampton Chronicle & Echo)*

40. Wesleys buses line up on the east side of Market Square in preparation for an old folks outing on Thursday 10 September 1964. Behind the buses is the monstrosity of a building erected to replace The Peacock Hotel.

Fortunately this building has now been demolished and replaced by the more acceptable Peacock Arcade. *(Northampton Chronicle & Echo)*

41. A typical view along the open-aired Peacock Way on Monday 8 March 1965. This thoroughfare led from the Market Square to Abington Street, lined each side with a variety of shops. Many people will remember the excellent cakes and pastries from Elisabeth the chef. The buildings are typical of the 1960s style – constructed with concrete and glass. *(Northampton Chronicle & Echo)*

42. When mini-skirts first came into fashion it was assumed the winter months would find them hanging in the wardrobe, but their owners proved to be hardy individuals. Braving the elements, this young lady sets out along Peacock Way for a night on the town on a cold and wet Friday 2 December 1966. *(Northampton Chronicle & Echo)*

43. A newly erected Town Guide attracts attention from the younger generation on Tuesday 7 September 1965. Situated opposite the entrance to Peacock Way, it was a useful facility for visitors to the town, but unfortunately it eventually had to be removed because of persistent vandalism. *(Northampton Chronicle & Echo)*

44. Political parties are always looking for new ways to attract votes, but not many ideas are as novel as this one, pictured on the Market Square during Friday 2 October 1959.
(Northampton Chronicle & Echo)

45. As well as normal everyday shoppers, various characters have turned up on the Market Square over the years. On Friday 5 April 1957 Rob Ruadh Mhacgregor called by en route to his home town of Dollar, 38 miles north of Edinburgh following a pilgrimage on foot to Canterbury and other places – a round trip of about 1000 miles. The soles of his shoes had tyre walls bonded on to them, and they showed very little sign of wear; which may be worth noting.
(Northampton Chronicle & Echo)

46. A local garage uses the Market for advertising purposes, displaying one of the new Vauxhall Vivas on Thursday 9 September 1971. The gentleman on the left is obviously admiring the rear of the model! *(Northampton Chronicle & Echo)*

47. Weather conditions were a lot different on Tuesday 9 January 1968 when a heavy fall of snow caused the usual traffic chaos. Fortunately for the motorist, passers-by and a policeman help to get him on the move.
(Northampton Chronicle & Echo)

48. Drum Lane – between the Market Square and Mercer's Row – has changed very little over the years, but this view is always impressive, with the tower of All Saints Church dominating the background. Here, on Saturday 12 April 1969, two young ladies, one resplendent in period costume, advertise the forthcoming *Mercury & Herald* beauty queen contest. *(Northampton Chronicle & Echo)*

AROUND ALL SAINTS

49. All Saints Church in 1953, the centrepiece of Northampton, and one of the most stately churches of its date outside London. It was rebuilt in Wrenn Style in 1680 after the great fire of 1675 had burned down all but the tower of the original church. Over the portico, which was added in 1701, stands a statue of King Charles II wearing a Roman toga and full-bottomed wig. It was he who gave 1000 tons of timber from local royal forests, and seven years remission of chimney money (a tax), to assist in the rebuilding of the church and part of the town – a gift that is recognized by an inscription over the full length of the portico. Because of this gesture, every year on 'Oak Apple Day' (29 May) an oak garland is traditionally placed on the statue by the verger of All Saints.
(Northampton Chronicle & Echo)

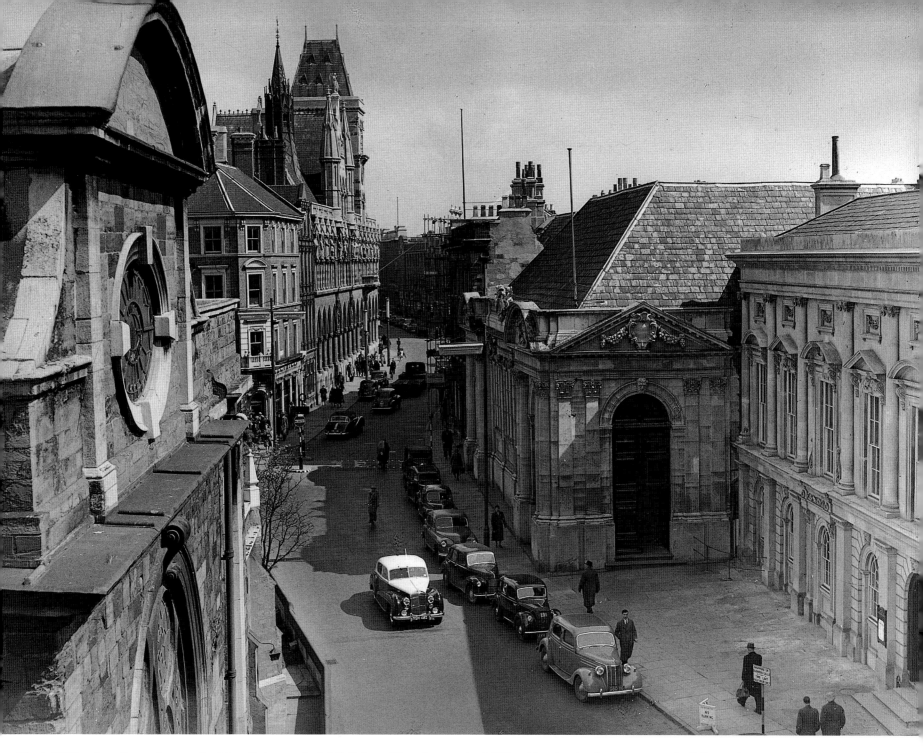

50. A 1950s view from the south side of the roof of All Saints Church looking along George Row into St Giles Square and beyond to St Giles Street. The superb architecture of the Town Hall dominates the background while to the right is the court building of Sessions House (built in 1678), said to be the first important building to be erected after the great fire of 1675. Next to this building, set back from the road, were the then County Council offices. *(Northampton Chronicle & Echo)*

51. A 1920s view of Wood Hill from Mercer's Row showing a wonderful array of cars parked adjacent to the public conveniences. At Adams Corner House on the corner of Wood Hill and St Giles Square during the 1950s there was a basement cafeteria called 'The Clipper' which was shaped and fitted out like the inside of an aeroplane fuselage.

52. A May 1963 view of the buildings on Wood Hill that have since been demolished. Perhaps the greatest loss to the people of the town was The Black Boy Hotel which had a reputation for excellent lunches, being well patronized by local townsfolk. *(Northampton Borough Council)*

53. (above) When Northampton man Frank Eckford lost a leg during the First World War the outlook appeared far from promising for him, but on the way through Paris during his return home he noticed the street newspaper kiosks, and this gave him an idea. He set up his first kiosk in 1919 in front of All Saints, shown above in the autumn of 1925. The tram in the picture was the first of the original electric trams to be refurbished, receiving a roof to the top deck early in 1924.
(Northampton Borough Council Archive)

54. (right) In 1926 the Eckfords moved their kiosk to Wood Hill and retained the pitch for many years thereafter. The picture on the right shows it as it was on Thursday 5 November 1953. At the end of 1953 they moved to their new mobile kiosk on Market Square (see picture 19). *(Northampton Chronicle & Echo)*

55. After war had been declared in September 1939, sandbag shelters were erected for the protection of essential service personnel. This one was built on the island at the junction of Mercer's Row and Wood Hill. The ARP (Air Raid Precautions) shelter that the notice points to was the underground toilets in Wood Hill. *(W.J.S. Meredith)*

56. Snow fell heavily on the morning of Thursday 5 March 1970 and, as usual, brought chaos to the roads of Northampton. This scene, looking down Mercer's Row towards All Saints, was photographed at lunchtime when conditions had improved. The bus inspectors' kiosk can be seen on the left-hand side with one of the Northampton Corporation buses (No. 225) parked ready for its next duty. (*Northampton Chronicle & Echo*)

57. On the corner of Abington Street and Wood Hill the premises of Spoor and Son have been vacated ready for demolition in preparation for the widening of the lower end of Abington Street in 1935. The Doffman building on the corner of Market Square and Abington Street was probably one of the first buildings to be rebuilt after the great fire in 1675, still retaining this date on a plaque fixed to the Abington Street side of the building. *(W.J.S. Meredith)*

58. Mercer's Row on a very wet Thursday 3 December 1931. Two Grose-bodied six-wheeler buses await their departure time, while one of the town's four single-decker trams (No. 37) prepares to leave for St James.

Not many photographers had the imagination and hardiness to take pictures in such weather, especially during the 1930s. *(W.J.S. Meredith)*

59. A wintry scene at dusk at the junction of Abington Street and the Market Square on Tuesday 12 January 1960. The Northampton Corporation bus (No. 206), with its destination board blotted out by snow, is turning into Wood Hill. On the far side of the Square the *Chronicle & Echo* building is ablaze with light on all floors, whilst at ground level the market stallholders brave the cold as they serve their customers under the light of their hissing Tilley lamps. Christmas decorations have yet to be removed, and note the RAC road sign to Sywell Aerodrome somewhat unusually situated on the lamp post in the middle of the town.
(Northampton Chronicle & Echo)

60. A busy scene in Mercer's Row during the summer of 1922, and not one person is without a hat! Both the trams waiting to move off along Abington Street are in original condition – No. 12 having been in the first batch bought during 1904. *(Pamlin Prints No. 72182)*

61. Another busy scene, this time at the bottom of the Drapery during late summer 1918 towards the end of the First World War, and there are a number of soldiers amongst the throng. The tram in the foreground, which still has its upper windows two-thirds blacked out, is one of the later ones. The other two are the earlier open-topped type. To the right of the picture, the lady walking purposefully towards the camera carrying a box in her right hand is one of the tram conductresses.
(Northampton Borough Council Archive)

62. Work progresses on the major repairs to the tram tracks at the Gold Street and Bridge Street junction on Saturday 2 September 1933. In the background, buses head for Weston and Far Cotton. The Far Cotton people were being spoilt at this time, being provided with comfortable buses to ride in, and there were many complaints when the rattling, bone-shaking trams returned to the route until their demise in December 1934. *(W.J.S. Meredith)*

63. The winter of 1947 was a particularly severe one, and the Northampton Borough Council pressed into service every available vehicle to assist with snow clearing – even this steam lorry seen here on duty outside All Saints Church. *(Northampton Borough Council Archive – Cyril Arnold)*

64. The Fire Brigade often gave a helping hand to Council workers if a ladder was required to reach difficult heights. Here we see an ancient Northampton based fire engine with a Leyland/Metz turntable, fitted with a special five-section ladder, being used for street light maintenance work.

This view, looking from Abington Street along Mercer's Row, was photographed on Thursday 27 October 1960. A Northampton Corporation bus (No. 170), built in 1949, waits to depart with the No. 11 service to Manfield Hospital. (*Northampton Chronicle & Echo*)

65. Considerable traffic congestion at the junction of Bridge Street, Gold Street and the Drapery on Friday 31 March 1967 as the local constabulary look on. Of interest is the electric hand-driven Royal Mail vehicle, Boots the chemists, Palmers the tailors and Hardys furniture store, still trading at the time, and they will be remembered by many Northamptonians. *(Northampton Chronicle & Echo)*

66. Viewed from under the portico to All Saints, the Lady Mayor, Ruth Perkins, and other dignitaries walk in procession towards the church to attend the Civic Sunday Service on 26 May 1968, the first Sunday after Mayor-making. *(Northampton Chronicle & Echo)*

67. Crowds gather outside All Saints Church to watch sentries from the Inkerman Company of the Grenadier Guards on Tuesday 25 September 1962. The Guardsmen were visiting the town on a recruiting drive and are seen here giving a demonstration of changing the guard in front of the portico. *(Northampton Chronicle & Echo)*

68. Tuesday 22 August 1967 provides a glimpse of a function under All Saints portico, with entertainment being provided by folk singers and coffee by the ladies. The hairstyles and dress of the couple in the alcove are typical of that era. *(Northampton Chronicle & Echo)*

69. Entertainment for the youngsters under All Saints portico on Saturday 4 July 1964 with the arrival of a 'Dalek', one of the originals used in the 'Dr Who' TV series which had been donated by the BBC to Dr Barnado's for raising funds – this day being a flag day collection. Two people from local organizations took it in turns to be inside the 'Dalek' for operational (and perhaps extermination?) purposes. *(Northampton Chronicle & Echo)*

HIGHWAYS AND BYWAYS
East from All Saints

70. An unusual vantage point from the top of the Boots building on the corner of Gold Street and the Drapery looking towards Mercer's Row and Abington Street in February 1960. The National Westminster Bank building on the left was built in 1928. All the buildings to the right of Burton's on Wood Hill have been rebuilt. *(Northampton Chronicle & Echo)*

71. A real look back into the past as we witness a parade of horses making their way up Abington Street adjacent to the track used for the passage of horse-drawn trams. The end-on building in the distance is The Old Duke of Clarence public house, later replaced by Waterloo House, on the corner of Mercer's Row and the Market Square. In Stanton's window one of the notices advertises Dallington Fête on Saturday 1 July 1893.
(Northampton Borough Council Archive)

72. A wander down Wood Street on Tuesday afternoon 15 February 1938 brings one to the junction of Abington Street and Fish Street. It was at this location 10 years earlier that Northampton's first set of traffic lights was installed. At the time the town was the third in the British Isles to have traffic lights. Although the building on the right, built in 1895, was later demolished, much of the rest of Fish Street remains. *(W.J.S. Meredith)*

73. Abington Street on Thursday 28 February 1963 at the junction with Wellington Street. The familiar sight of the Gas Board building built in 1940 dominated this part of the street for almost 30 years. Alas, like a number of landmarks in Abington Street, it was to disappear in years to come. The British Home Stores building was also modernized. Street parking, not only in Abington Street but also Wellington Street, was still the norm in those days, as was the two-way traffic. *(Northampton Chronicle & Echo)*

74. A superb panorama looking down Abington Street towards the town centre during June 1922 shows two buildings that are sadly no longer part of the scene. On the left is the New Theatre, opened in 1912 and demolished during 1960, while on the right is the Notre Dame High School which, including the fine chapel at the rear, was demolished in 1979. (Both these buildings are looked at in more detail in this book's companion volume). Tram No. 13 makes steady progress towards Abington Square, but there's not much chance of it catching up with the pony and trap. *(Pamlin Prints No. 72173)*

75. A typical view of Abington Street seen from the Gas Board building during December 1953. There are some splendid examples of vehicles of the era, and the buildings display their differing styles of architecture. Fortunately, the four nearest structures were to survive the ravages of modernization. The Central Library was built in 1910 and the Co-op Arcade opened in 1938. The New Theatre situated above the lorry to the left of the picture had five more years of presenting performances before being demolished in 1960. *(Northampton Chronicle & Echo)*

76. A unique view of the 2000-seater Savoy cinema on the corner of Lower Mounts and Abington Square as it nears completion on Friday 24 April 1936. At the time the building was considered to be of a very modern appearance with its typical 1930s style of architecture. *(W.J.S. Meredith)*

77. Another view of the Savoy cinema from York Road. It must have looked quite a sight for the 1930s with both neon and flood lighting! At this time in April 1937 it was also decorated for the forthcoming Coronation of King George VI on 12 May. *(L. Hanson)*

78. A glimpse inside the ABC (Savoy) cinema on Wednesday 22 December 1965 finds a Hillman Imp languishing in the foyer. This was used in connection with a crime prevention display put on by Northampton Police. Outside the notice board informs the public that Pathe News has made yet another major scoop. (*Northampton Chronicle & Echo*)

79. They must have liked cars at the ABC (Savoy), for an even more amazing sight was this promotional gimmick for the new Riley Elf Mk III. Restrained by ropes, the car sits precariously on the stairs leading from the cinema foyer on Friday 27 January 1967. Today's safety regulations certainly wouldn't allow main exits to be blocked like this.
(*Northampton Chronicle & Echo*)

80. To commemorate the 16th anniversary of the setting up of the ABC Minors, the cinema management had a cake baked and also decided to support the Mayor of Northampton's 'Coal Fund for the Elderly' ready for Christmas 1963. At a spot in the foyer, designated the coal collection point, a posed group of Minors look on as the scheme is launched on Saturday 30 November 1963. (*Northampton Chronicle & Echo*)

81. This view, photographed on Wednesday 8 July 1964 from the top of the building in Lower Mounts, shows a splendid panoramic view of Abington Square and Wellingborough Road. Little demolition and modernization had actually taken place in this particular area. The ABC cinema remains the only cinema in use in the town centre. Northampton Corporation bus No. 205 waits at the traffic lights with its destination blind already changed to indicate the No. 12 service from the town centre to Dallington Green. St Edmund's Church tower stands out on the horizon in the middle of the landscape view. The church, along with its tower, was demolished in 1979 for road widening, leaving the graveyard. *(Northampton Chronicle & Echo)*

82. Abington Square at the junction of the Kettering and Wellingborough roads photographed during the morning rush hour on Friday 15 May 1959 showing two-way operation of traffic on both roads. Northampton Corporation and United Counties buses bring commuters into the town, and schoolgirls prepare to walk the short distance to Notre Dame School in Abington Street. This junction always proved to be a bottleneck, and not surprisingly traffic jams were frequent. Charles Bradlaugh's statue remains dominant in the centre of the picture, while above this and the roof of the Central Hall, the tower of St Giles Church can just be seen. *(Northampton Chronicle & Echo)*

83. (above) An intriguing view of Abington Square circa 1906 finds tram No. 6 steadily making its way towards the town centre from the Kettering Road direction. To the right of the tram is the familiar statue of Charles Bradlaugh standing in front of the building once known as the People's Café, but when this photograph was taken it had become a leather warehouse and billiards hall. The building was demolished during the early 1930s, part of the site later being occupied by the Garden of Remembrance. *(Northampton Borough Council Archive)*

84.(facing page) Moving into Kettering Road, tram No. 31 (one of the later type with closed in upper deck) trundles round the curve past Raglan Street heading for Kingsley on Friday 6 June 1930. The trams were withdrawn from this route during September the same year. As in the previous photograph, the large pair of eyes on the tram advertises R.H. Primavesi, one of the local opticians. Queensgrove Methodist Church can be seen in the distance on the corner of Grove Road. All the buildings on the right have long been demolished. *(W.J.S. Meredith)*

85. How pleasant to see the Kettering Road looking quiet and traffic-free on Thursday 24 June 1971. This view, looking towards the town centre, shows the Queensgrove Methodist Church surrounded by scaffolding while two long-established Northampton firms – Jones and Caves – are on the right. Although the right-hand side of the street remains largely unchanged, all the buildings on the left-hand side have now disappeared. *(Northampton Chronicle & Echo)*

86. The famous White Elephant landmark at the junction of Kingsley Road, Abington Grove, Kingsley Park Terrace and East Park Parade is known by many Northamptonians. The Victorian building was erected in 1883 as The Kingsley Park Hotel to accommodate the many visitors to the horse races at the nearby Racecourse. Alas, when the course was closed in 1904 the remote hotel literally became a 'white elephant' and the name has remained ever since. In recent years it has been a pub and, but for a brief period, still calls itself the White Elephant, and the junction has taken this name. The elephant sign, though, seen here in this early 1970s photograph, has disappeared. *(John Denton)*

87. To many Northamptonians living in the Kingsley area, the spire of St Matthew's Church has been a familiar landmark. However, how many have wondered what the view from the spire offers? Here are two superb panoramic scenes photographed on the morning of Wednesday 29 October 1958 in perfect autumnal conditions. The architecture of the buildings in Kingsley Park Terrace is gloriously enhanced by the low autumn lighting.

Coal fires were still the order of the day, as can be seen from the smoke rising from a number of chimneys. A Northampton Transport bus on the No. 15 service to the Headlands passes by, as a few early shoppers start their day. On the right of the photograph at the corner of Milton Street, Kingsley Park Methodist Church stands proud.
(Northampton Chronicle & Echo)

88. The second view looks along the Kettering Road towards Spinney Hill and shows the residential area of Kingsley Park. The very small number of vehicles parked or travelling on the road shows that the era of widespread car ownership was yet to come. Scenes like this were commonplace in the 1950s, and one hopes that one day they may return.
(Northampton Chronicle & Echo)

89. A policeman stands on point duty in the narrow part of Wellingborough Road directing traffic from Raglan Street towards Abington Square on a wet and miserable Tuesday 5 December 1961. During 1967 all the left side of Wellingborough Road that is in view between Raglan Street and St Edmund's Hospital was demolished to make way for the new dual carriageway. *(Northampton Chronicle & Echo)*

90. One of Northampton's most serious fires for years occurred on Saturday 8 August 1959 when the factory of greetings card manufacturers Giesen and Wolff, situated in St Edmund's Road, went up in flames. At the height of the fire there were 80 firemen and 15 appliances on the scene, and people from houses in adjacent streets were evacuated as a precaution. *(Northampton Borough Council Archive)*

91. Many Northamptonians who were motor cyclists in the good old days will remember the Stokes shop and its owner Norman Stokes. Here he poses outside his shop in Wellingborough Road on Monday 8 April 1957 with no less than 27 new Lambretta scooters ready for sale. The scooters had earlier arrived by train from Italy and were delivered to his premises by one of the many BR 'mechanical horses'. Vernon Street, with its Victorian terraced houses, was to change dramatically in the years to come. *(Northampton Chronicle & Echo)*

92. In direct contrast to the scooters on the opposite page, Norman Clarke's furniture store at the junction of Palmerston Road and Wellingborough Road, on Wednesday 21 September 1966, has a display of 17 armchairs for sale. How fashions have changed in the last 30 years! One assumes the shop staff are keeping an eye on the weather, just in case it starts raining. *(Northampton Chronicle & Echo)*

93. Traffic leaves York Road and heads towards Lower Mounts at the junction with Abington Street on Thursday 19 July 1962. York Road was later to be widened with the demolition of the two buildings on the right-hand side in Abington Street. (*Northampton Chronicle & Echo*)

94. Road accidents have always occurred, and these two pictures show lorries having problems at two well known locations in the town. This one (left) shows an overturned Vernon Packaging lorry in Campbell Street, with Campbell Square at the top of the road. Bailiff Street can be seen going off to the left. The date is 4 July 1967. The large building at the top of the hill used to be Campbell Square School but this, together with the other buildings, has since been demolished. Fortunately no one was in the car crushed by the lorry. *(Northampton Chronicle & Echo)*

95. (below) By a stroke of good fortune no one was waiting in the vicinity of the bus stop at Lower Mounts when this lorry, loaded with an earth-moving vehicle, toppled over at 5 p.m. on Monday 19 July 1965 at the busy Abington Street/Upper Mounts/York Road junction. York Road by this time had already been widened. The fire service is in attendance because of diesel spillage. *(Northampton Chronicle & Echo)*

96. A nostalgic elevated look towards the fire station from the corner of Abington Street on Wednesday 8 July 1964 shows a scene that was to change dramatically in years to come. The view is along Lower Mounts to Upper Mounts, and there's just a glimpse of Lady's Lane on the left-hand side. Pupils from the St Mary's Infant School gather to go back to their classrooms after mid-morning break. Meanwhile, over the school wall there's barely any traffic on the road. On the right at the corner of Overstone Road the splendid building belonging to shoe manufacturers Parker and Tearl stands proud – one of the many superb landmarks in the town centre that should have been listed and preserved instead of being demolished.

(Northampton Chronicle & Echo)

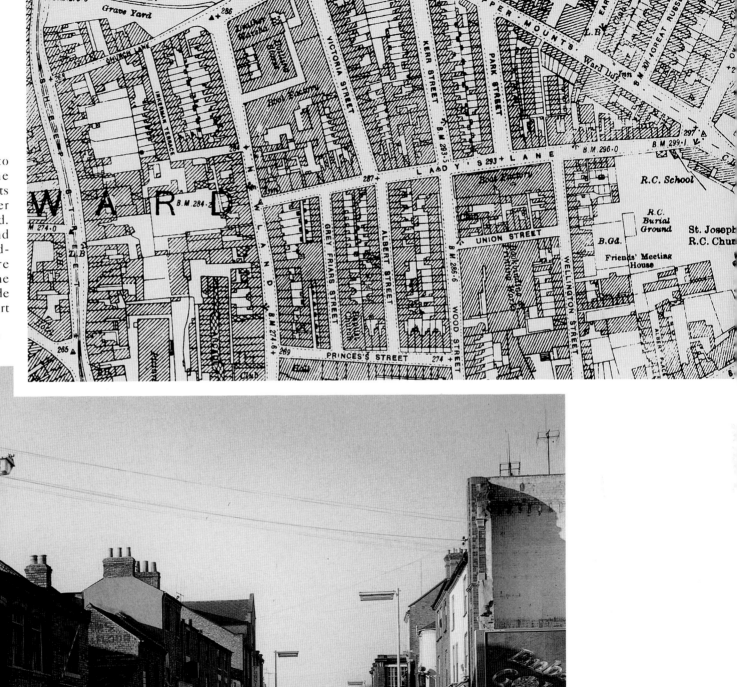

97. From the entrance to Overstone Road, this scene looking towards Upper Mounts on Wednesday 23 December 1970 is surprisingly deserted. Where are all the people and cars, considering it's mid-afternoon two days before Christmas? Before long all the buildings on the left-hand side were to be demolished as part of the modernization plan.
(Northampton Borough Council)

98. Sun streams through the smoke haze from the coal fires in the dwellings of Mounts Gardens as neighbours pass the time of day with a chat on Sunday 17 October 1965. Mounts Gardens was situated to the rear of the houses on the east side of Park Street, with pedestrian access only to the dwellings on either side. Viewed from Upper Mounts, a lady and child stroll gently towards Lady's Lane in this scene of old Northampton. *(Robin Puryer)*

99. The first multi-storey car park to be built in Northampton at the rear of the ABC cinema was officially opened by the Mayor on Saturday 12 August 1967. Looking on are councillors and officers of the Borough Engineer's Department as the Mayor's car passes under the barrier. The cost of parking was 6d per hour (minimum 1s, maximum 5s). Behind the Mayor's car and across the road is the ornate factory of Parker and Tearl that used to stand on the corner of Overstone Road. The other frontage is the shop premises of leather merchants E.R. Bush that stood at the junction of Lady's Lane and Upper Mounts. Even the multi-storey car park itself has since been demolished. *(Northampton Chronicle & Echo)*

100. How fortunate that these views from the top of the fire station building were photographed before the whole area was transformed. In this view of the houses in Park Street in March 1971 signs of the things to come can be seen by some of the houses already being boarded up prior to demolition. In the background the huge former Randall's shoe manufacturing building stands in Lady's Lane, with Northampton Power Station's cooling towers prominent on the horizon. The car park area at the rear of the houses in Park Street was previously the location of Mounts Gardens, seen in picture 98. *(Northampton Borough Council)*

101. This rooftop scene was photographed on Thursday 19 November 1959. The Victorian terraced houses along Kerr Street back on to similar examples in Park Street. A remarkable picture showing the dramatic landscape of Northampton in those days, and the close proximity of residential houses to the centre of the town. Kerr Street, along with others leading to the Police and Fire stations, vanished in 1972. *(Northampton Chronicle & Echo)*

102. Another tremendous panoramic view of the centre of Northampton, looking down Kerr Street which leads into Wood Street, photographed in March 1971. It's almost unbelievable that so much of this scene, that was Northampton as many Northamptonians remember it, was to completely disappear. On the horizon the Guildhall (centre) and All Saints (to the right) dominate. *(Northampton Borough Council)*

103. A dramatic view along Wellington Street, leading on to Abington Street, photographed on Wednesday 23 December 1970. The street was used by many as a through way from Lady's Lane. Deserted here, with just one solitary car, the variety of architecture on the many different buildings is accentuated by the low December sun. *(Northampton Borough Council)*

104. Looking across from the Fire Station in Upper Mounts and down Church Lane, the sight of St Sepulchre's Church dominates the picture. In the distance the tower of St Andrew's Church is visible, and on the left the Horton and Arlidge warehouse, with its tall recessed Italianate tower, that was later to be demolished along with the houses in the foreground. In the background the two multi-storey blocks of flats had already been on the Northampton skyline for eight years in this 1971 photograph.
(*Northampton Borough Council*)

105. Another rooftop view from the opposite side to that of picture 104 from the spire of St Sepulchre's Church on Friday 23 October 1953. The whole scene has that nostalgic look of the 1950s about it, and this is further enhanced by the smoke from the chimneys of the many homes in the picture. The plain architecture of the Campbell Square Police Station and Fire Station contrasts strikingly with that of the Horton and Arlidge building on the right. Much of the housing behind the Police and Fire stations remains untouched, but on the right-hand side, although Victoria Street still exists, all the buildings have been demolished.
(Northampton Chronicle & Echo)

HIGHWAYS AND BYWAYS
Down past the Guildhall

106. Outside the Guildhall on Thursday 27 October 1966 the Union Jack flies at half mast to mark the official day of mourning for the victims of the Aberfan tragedy. The previous week a coal pit waste tip slid on to this South Wales mining village engulfing homes and a school, claiming many lives, including those of 116 children trapped in their classrooms. The single storey shops opposite have now been demolished revealing the stone buildings behind. *(Northampton Chronicle & Echo)*

107. A deserted St Giles Square on the evening of Monday 23 October 1961 has given the photographer an opportunity to capture the magnificent architecture of the Town Hall. The building was constructed in two parts. The first part (the right-hand side when facing the building) was designed by Mr E.W. Godwin and opened in 1864. The second part was designed by Matthew Holding and was opened in 1892. The Mayor's limousine stands outside together with chauffeur in this superb nocturnal study. *(Northampton Chronicle & Echo)*

108. It's just after 10 a.m. on Saturday 31 January 1959 and the early morning shoppers are already out. This elevated view of St Giles Street shows that the two-way traffic is sparse and that parking was allowed on both sides of the street at the time. The buildings on the right from the Town Hall up St Giles Street were to disappear in later years, as were the shops in front of the Town Hall in St Giles Square. *(Northampton Chronicle & Echo)*

109. A look up Derngate towards St Giles Square on Friday 22 November 1968 reveals a row of shops that Northamptonians would remember well – Robertsons the confectioners, Kings the butcher, Harry Bowler, greengrocer and florist – all to disappear with the coming of the Derngate Centre. The Swan Hotel was later to become a pub and was renamed the Mailcoach. On the far right-hand side is Montague Jeffrey's store on the corner of St Giles Street – another established Northampton landmark. *(Northampton Chronicle & Echo)*

110. An elevated glimpse of Derngate looking towards the Northampton Power Station on Monday 1 May 1961. The United Counties Bus Station is on the right with the café that many Northamptonians will remember in the middle of the picture. To many it was known as the green Bus Station as, of course, United Counties buses arrived and departed. Also all the long-distance coach services used this Bus Station, which the Derngate Centre was subsequently to replace, with the buses going to Greyfriars. *(Northampton Chronicle & Echo)*

111. Those were the days at the Bus Station in Derngate when queues used to go all the way up Derngate towards the Town Hall as people waited for their buses. This 1939 scene shows the start of the town's summer holidays and it looks like bus travel was as popular as rail travel. The familiar Enquiry and Booking Office for the Bus Station is directly behind the queue of people. *(W.J.S. Meredith)*

112. Chaos inside the United Counties Bus Station on Thursday 9 February 1961. Commuters and school children mingle amongst the many buses, wondering what services will actually be running. A strike was taking place at the time, and bus drivers and conductors can be seen gathered on the left deciding what action to take next! There is also a *Chronicle & Echo* van on the scene as the buses were used to distribute copies of the newspaper to agents both in the town and surrounding countryside in those days. *(Northampton Chronicle & Echo)*

113. The start of the factory fortnight, and Northamptonians are off on their holidays. This view on Saturday 15 July 1967 shows single decker coaches waiting to leave for Eastbourne, Margate/Ramsgate and Hastings, and no doubt their passengers are anxious to get to their destinations as soon as possible. *(Northampton Chronicle & Echo)*

114. On Monday 11 May 1964 a fitter was returning an empty United Counties bus to the Houghton Road garage (actually on the Bedford Road). As he pulled out from the Bus Station he had to swerve to avoid a cyclist and ended up becoming firmly wedged under the canopy of the recently constructed New Wilton House. *(Northampton Chronicle & Echo)*

115. The main concern during recovery was that the bus might tip over on its side while being pulled clear of the building. It was therefore decided, as a precautionary measure, to position a single-decker alongside. Fortun-ately the single-decker was not needed as a support, and recovery was satisfactorily completed without further mishap.
(Northampton Chronicle & Echo)

HIGHWAYS AND BYWAYS
Heading for St James

116. This fascinating view of Gold Street was photographed from the roof of All Saints Church during 1953. Fortunately the view remains generally unchanged as far as the buildings are concerned. The magnificent architecture of the building on the right, occupied by Boots the chemists since 1905, stands out splendidly. Other landmarks in Gold Street, such as the Grand Hotel which opened in 1891, are visible. The two-way traffic system was still in operation here, as with many streets in the town centre. *(Northampton Chronicle & Echo)*

117. A murky haze hangs in the lower part of Gold Street as a tram begins its journey towards St James circa 1915. The high-pitched roof of the corner tower to The Queen's Head public house on the Gold Street/ College Street corner can just be seen – another ornate Northampton building lost to demolition during 1961. *(Northampton Borough Council Archive)*

118. It's that time of the year again and, with holidays looming, a happy group of Northamptonians forms a queue on Saturday 11 July 1959 outside the Frames Tours office on the corner of Gold Street and Kingswell Street. This remarkable small office was a hive of activity, and tickets for trips both in the UK and overseas were being issued. Of course, there were no computers in those days and each ticket was written out by hand. The signs outside the bureau are interesting in their own right, especially the one on the corner of the building stating that 'LMS railway tickets are issued here' despite the fact that the LMS ceased in December 1947. Also of interest is the ornate wrought iron decoration outside the first-floor window. Six months after this photograph was taken the site was taken over by Bowen and Collins, two former Cobblers players, who set up a sports shop, while the Frames Tours office moved to larger premises. *(Northampton Chronicle & Echo)*

119. A mid-afternoon look at Gold Street on Friday 20 July 1962 reveals a scene that has remained remarkably similar over the years, except that many of the shops have changed ownership. The varied examples of buildings remain, with the exception of the tall building next to the Civic store. This was demolished and replaced with a modern structure to house Brierley's store. Many Northamptonians will remember the Woolworth's store, Swann's and, of course, John Lever's record shop that graced Gold Street for many years. *(Northampton Chronicle & Echo)*

121. (above) Stepping inside R.L. Capell's we are greeted by an amazing array of implements, from hand water pumps and hand ploughs to shotguns, beehives and two-stroke engines – the variety seems endless. *(Northampton Borough Council Archive)*

120. (facing page) Hardware of every type and description decorates the windows of R.L. Capell in Gold Street in this scene photographed during the early 1900s. The shop frontage is unusual in that it has both ground floor and first floor display windows. *(Northampton Borough Council Archive)*

122. (facing page) Marefair in September 1954 from the roof of Bell's premises in Gold Street. It is interesting to see the old cobbled surface showing through the light asphalt coating. All the buildings on the right-hand side have now gone, as has The Shakespeare public house which was lost with the widening of Horse Shoe Street. *(Northampton Chronicle & Echo)*

123. (above) A flag-bedecked and crowded Marefair and Gold Street, minutes after Her Majesty the Queen had passed by during her visit to the town on Friday 9 July 1965. Many changes have since occurred in Marefair, and all the left-hand side was eventually demolished. *(Robin Puryer)*

124. Marefair looking up Gold Street during 1914 finds a busy scene delightfully free from motorized transport. The only car in sight is parked on the right up Gold Street. Carcases are being unloaded from a horse-drawn wagon into the open-fronted butchers shop on the corner of Horsemarket as other people go about their daily business. On the far left a trap stands outside the North Western Railway Company's North Western Hotel. Vint's Palace was opened in September 1913 for both film shows and variety acts, and remained in business for six years. *(Northampton Borough Council Archive)*

125. A similar view towards Gold Street photographed from the opposite side of the road outside The North Western Hotel in May 1937. The Majestic theatre (previously Vint's Palace) had been so named for the past 17 years but was in its last year of operation. The Daimler bus, by contrast, was almost brand new and the first of a batch of six delivered to Northampton Corporation Transport in April 1937. It is interesting to see that Marefair is fully covered by tarmac at this time, but that in the 1954 view in picture 122 the old cobbled surface had begun to show through. *(W.J.S. Meredith)*

126. No. 1, the first electric tram to be bought by Northampton Corporation Tramways in 1904, makes its way past St Peter's churchyard towards St James some time during 1914. The unusual sight of a camera attracts attention from passers by making their way from Black Lion Hill towards Marefair past Propert's Commercial Hotel on the corner of Chalk Lane. Grose's garage sign can be seen in Marefair, the firm having established itself in the premises during 1912.
(Northampton Borough Council Archive)

127. An interesting view from Castle Station yard on Saturday 8 April 1939 with Manning's Castle Brewery on Black Lion Hill opposite the yard entrance. Behind the wooden refreshments shed on the left, called the Coffee Tavern, is Pickfords Depository which in earlier times was Warner's Hotel, and before that a school. The car being used as a taxi is a rather uncommon Belgian Minerva. It is parked in front of an advertisement for the Exchange cinema in The Parade, later to become known as the Gaumont. (W.J.S. Meredith)

128. This outstanding photograph, taken from the top of the St Katherine's Court building on Sunday 4 August 1957, gives an excellent panoramic view of the landscape looking towards Hunsbury Hill. The briefest of glimpses of Dorridge Street and Chalk Lane in the foreground lead down to St Peter's Church and an array of buildings in Marefair and Black Lion Hill. Many familiar landmarks appear in the picture, most of which have now disappeared, and to complete the scene a 4F class 0-6-0 brings a train into Castle Station from Peterborough, having run past the carriage sheds. The railway from Northampton Castle to Euston can be seen running out of the town over 15-arches viaduct and past the buildings of Airflow Streamlines Company. With the relentless expansion of Northampton, nearly all the fields in this picture have now been built on. *(W.J.S. Meredith)*

129. Another fascinating panoramic view from the top of the St Katherine's Court building, this time in the direction of St James's End. In the foreground are the rooftops of homes in Chalk Lane and Fitzroy Street. Northampton Castle Station is on the left, with the station platforms stretching the length of the picture, and the huge railway warehouse in the middle of the view. A 4F class 0-6-0 stands at the platform having just arrived with a train from Peterborough. The 'Dover' chimney at the cycle works was a landmark in the area, the same as the Express Lifts tower was to be in later years. *(W.J.S. Meredith)*

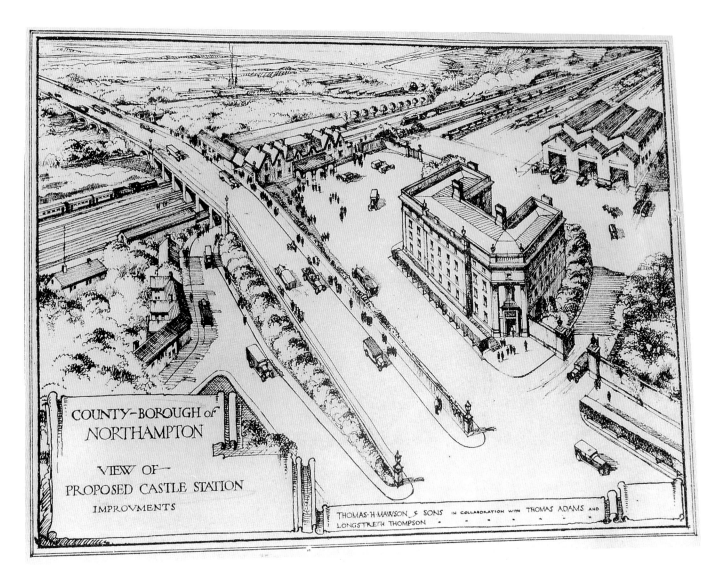

COUNTY-BOROUGH of
NORTHAMPTON

VIEW OF
PROPOSED CASTLE STATION

IMPROVMENTS

THOMAS H MAWSON & SONS IN COLLABORATION WITH THOMAS ADAMS AND LONGSTRETH THOMPSON

130. This illustration is rather intriguing as it shows an architect's drawing for proposed improvements to the Castle Station area of Northampton as early as March 1959. Unfortunately, the proposals were not carried out and instead the town ended up with a modern monstrosity. *(Northampton Chronicle & Echo)*

131. (above) This view from Black Lion Hill was photographed on Wednesday 12 July 1939. Gas lamps still lit the street and, but for the car on the bridge, the only vehicles present seem to be taxis in the station forecourt. A lone cyclist heads towards West Bridge and St James's Road. Also of note is the poster advertising the latest show at the New Theatre. (*W.J.S. Meredith*)

132. (below) An alternative view, photographed from the railway warehouse adjacent to the Station on Saturday 31 January 1959. A wonderful collection of vehicles is parked in the station car park, while a plume of steam near the bus on West Bridge suggests a train has just departed. (*Northampton Chronicle & Echo*)

133. The familiar entrance to Northampton Castle Station sees Northamptonians rushing for their tickets on Saturday 23 July 1966 with the town factory fortnight holiday just beginning. Over the years many youngsters and a good many adults have felt great excitement when entering Castle Station's ticket office as it gave access to a whole new world outside Northampton. *(Northampton Chronicle & Echo)*

134. With tickets purchased, passengers would make their way on to the platforms to await their trains. Until the early 1960s steam-hauled trains were the order of the day, and in this picture, photographed in the summer of 1958, the 10.27 a.m. (Saturday only) train to Wolverhampton stops at Platform 6 with rebuilt Royal Scot class No. 46155 THE LANCER at the head of the train. With train travel more commonplace during this era, trips to London to see an evening show were a regular occurrence amongst Northamptonians. A poster on the platform advertises Sandy Wilson's hit musical 'The Boy Friend' playing in its fifth year at the time at Wyndham's Theatre. *(C. Lucas)*

135. Not only family groups went away on holiday by train in the 1950s, but also school groups. In this happy scene on Platform 1 a group of schoolchildren from Daventry await their train to London in anticipation of a trip to Switzerland on Friday 29 July 1955. *(Northampton Chronicle & Echo)*

136. Many family partings and reunions would have been witnessed by Northampton Castle Station over the years. Here, on Friday 16 October 1953, the family of Dr and Mrs Stanley Thomas gather round to say goodbye to them and their two children, Judith and Susan, as they prepare for the first stage of a return journey to India where they would be carrying out hospital work in the Kond Hills. *(Northampton Chronicle & Echo)*

137. Once on to the train the Daventry school-party seen in picture 135 soon find their reserved coach, and some of the children have time to pose for the photographer before the train leaves for London. *(Northampton Chronicle & Echo)*

138. To many railway enthusiasts at Northampton the view of London-bound trains from the vantage point of West Bridge will long be remembered. However, how many of them recognize this view? The photographer's use of a long telephoto lens has pulled in the spire of St Mary's Church in Far Cotton and the immense gas holder so that they appear to loom over the carriage sheds. Meanwhile, rebuilt Royal Scot class No. 46114 COLDSTREAM GUARDSMAN, in poor external condition, heads towards Blisworth as the weekend diversions have overlapped into Monday 27 March 1961. *(Northampton Chronicle & Echo)*

139. There was a one-day strike of British Railway workers on Wednesday 3 October 1962, and here a group of NUR members share a light-hearted moment outside Northampton station. As always, it is the travelling public who suffer, and the disruption would have been the greater then when fewer people owned cars. *(Northampton Chronicle & Echo)*

140. Trolley loads of strike-bound goods stand neglected on Platform 1, deserted but for a policeman on the far right-hand side. Even under normal circumstances Platform 1 was well known for being littered with trolleys, but this day there will be some disappointed customers, and the perishable goods will have lost their value. There's no trace now of the station as seen here, as it was totally demolished in the mid-1960s.
(Northampton Chronicle & Echo)

141. The junction of the Weedon and Harlestone Roads on the morning of Thursday 8 January 1959 and schoolchildren are on their way to St James's School in Althorp Road. The clock on the tower of St James's Parish Church suggests it is 9.05 a.m. on this cold wintry morning. The tower was added to the church after the First World War as a memorial to one of the Grose family who lived nearby in Weedon Road. The tower's tubular bells, instead of the more traditional type, are unique to the area. The National Provincial Bank building on the corner of Althorp Road still exists, although the clock has disappeared. Althorp Café used to occupy this site in years gone by, and the road junction used to be known as Café Square. *(Northampton Chronicle & Echo)*

142. One of the single-decker Thorneycroft buses purchased by Northampton Corporation Transport in 1924 picks up passengers at the bottom of Sandhill Road, opposite the old Mettoy factory on Harlestone Road during the late 1920s. Originally fitted with solid tyres, it had by this time been converted to pneumatic ones, no doubt to the relief of the passengers. *(Northampton Borough Council Archive)*

143. (above) One of local haulier C. Butt's drivers has parked his low-loader on Spencer Bridge Road at the junction with Baring Road while calling in at the main depot on Wednesday 23 August 1961. His load is 1941-built 28-ton standard gauge industrial steam locomotive No. 109, en route from Risley in Yorkshire, where it had been in service at the Royal Navy Works Department, to a destination in Brackley. (*Northampton Chronicle & Echo*)

144. (facing page top) The St Andrews Road/Grafton Street/Spencer Bridge Road junction has changed in recent years. This view on Thursday 8 January 1959 shows traffic coming from Regent Square, heading towards Kings Heath, and a tanker about to climb up Grafton Street. Later road widening led to the demolition of all the buildings on both sides of the road. (*Northampton Chronicle & Echo*)

145. (facing page bottom) Another landmark to have recently disappeared is that of the Mettoy building in Harlestone Road, but the Northampton Co-op building still stands. Taken on Monday 7 March 1960, the photograph looks towards the A428 to Rugby. (*Northampton Chronicle & Echo*)

HIGHWAYS AND BYWAYS
Far Cotton foray

146. (facing page) A view down a rain-soaked Bridge Street in February 1960 photographed from the building that used to house Boots the chemist. Bridge Street, like Gold Street, has altered very little over the years. *(Northampton Chronicle & Echo)*

147. (above) A full-scale blizzard is under way in this December 1939 photograph taken from outside the Angel Hotel in Bridge Street looking towards the brewery at the far end of the street. The Angel Hotel is the sole surviving ancient inn in Northampton. *(W.J.S. Meredith)*

148. A view from the other end of Bridge Street looking up towards the junction with Gold Street on the afternoon of Monday 4 April 1960. Many of the buildings on the left have survived, even though the shops have changed owners. Of note are the two Coldham's shops, one on the right under the clock and the other across the road. Although there are plenty of parked cars, the only moving traffic in this picture is a solitary bicycle. *(Northampton Chronicle & Echo)*

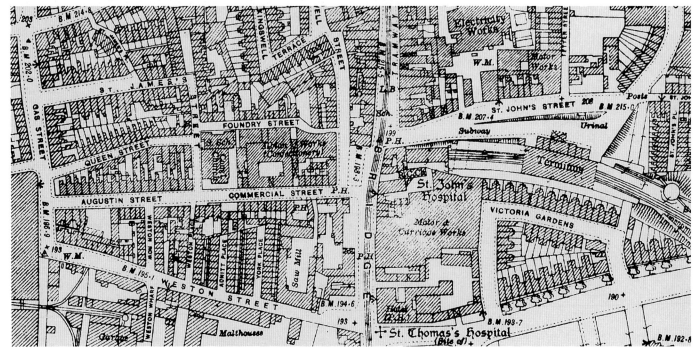

149. In an effort to 'Make Safe Cycling a Habit' members of the Invicta Cycling Club, to the amazement of onlookers, show how it shouldn't be done as three of them, in strange garb, wobble up Bridge Street on ancient bikes purposely breaking the 'rules' (including leaning on the lorry) to make their point on Saturday 24 October 1953.
(Northampton Chronicle & Echo)

150. A Northampton Corporation bus makes its way along Weston Street on a sunny day in May 1937 passing, on the left, the brewery malt houses with their strangely shaped ventilation cowls and, on the right, the old saw mills. Most striking in the picture, however, are the posters. At this time advertisements such as these were a common sight all over town. Weston Street was reconstructed as a dual carriageway during 1959/60 and renamed St Peter's Way (see picture 163) *(W.J.S. Meredith)*

151. Another view of old Northampton during May 1937 as a bus heads along Commercial Street into Augustin Street, both of which ran roughly parallel to Weston Street (shown opposite). The terraced houses on the left are constructed of sandstone blocks instead of the usual brick. At the end of the road on the other side of Bridge Street can be seen the old St John's Hospital building, first constructed in 1138 and altered around 300 years later. *(W.J.S. Meredith)*

152. From the Plough Hotel traffic can be seen queuing along Bridge Street by the old NBC brewery on a wet Friday 29 July 1966. This was one of a number of junctions in the town notorious for traffic congestion. The brewery buildings were completely replaced by the new Carlsberg Brewery in 1973. (*Northampton Chronicle & Echo*)

153. By way of comparison, here is the same view on Monday 17 March 1947. The flood, one of the worst in the town, resulted from a rapid thaw of very deep snow following one of the most severe winters on record. The traffic threads its way gingerly through the water as it heads towards South Bridge, and water can be seen gushing out of pipes at the entrance to the brewery as it is pumped out of the premises.
(Northampton Chronicle & Echo)

154. The River Nene was in flood, and water had spread across Foot Meadow and into the streets nearby, as can be seen in this picture taken from Tanner Street looking up Mill Lane on Monday 17 March 1947. In the distance is Gas Street, as yet unflooded, and a lonely pedestrian pensively picks his way towards the dry land. He *is* wearing Wellington boots, isn't he! *(Northampton Chronicle & Echo)*

155. On the same day a look along Victoria Promenade reveals another flooded street. The railway bridge that carried the Midland Railway line from St John's Street Station to Bedford can be seen in the distance with a rake of wagons surprisingly parked in view. The floodwater has no doubt spread across the Cattle Market (to the right of this picture) and the surrounding area, being unable to drain away into the river.
(Northampton Chronicle & Echo)

156. St John's Station opened in 1872 as Northampton's third railway station, and remained in business until its closure in July 1939. The station was situated at the bottom of Guildhall Road and was the nearest one to the town centre. For over 20 years it stood derelict before being demo-lished in 1960. Its car park was used quite often by people visiting the town, as this photograph shows. Sadly its unusual architecture wasn't considered enough for a preservation order. *(Robin Puryer)*

157. The dismal sight of the remains of St John's Street Station after demolition on Saturday 31 December 1960. Two boys clamber over the remains of the portico columns. What would the Midland Railway builders have thought to see all their work destroyed – sheer vandalism! When the site had been cleared it was used for the inevitable car park. *(Northampton Chronicle & Echo)*

158. This superbly composed photograph showing the unique sight of a railway arch overlooking a Northampton street was taken on Tuesday 21 January 1958. The location is under the St John's Street Station platforms and the Victorian buildings in view are located in Victoria Gardens, with Victoria Promenade in the background. Although the railway arch and gas lamp have now gone, the scene is remarkably similar but one that many Northamptonians still never notice! *(Northampton Chronicle & Echo)*

159. No doubt livestock have been driven along Victoria Promenade many times over the years, but it was a pleasurable experience to witness such a rural scene as late as Tuesday 25 August 1964. The cattle are just passing the Cattle Market and are making their way towards Bedford Road, probably for the meadows adjacent to the River Nene.
(Northampton Chronicle & Echo)

160. Livestock was auctioned off at the town's Market Square until the opening of the new Cattle Market on 17 July 1873. Here in this view, 80 years later, is a scene that would have changed little over the years at the Cattle Market, with the auctioning of rams and ewes well under way as the time approaches 11.06 a.m. on a dull morning during the early 1950s. *(Northampton Chronicle & Echo)*

161. (left) Farmers obviously enjoy the markets, not only for the business but also the opportunity to chat with other farmers from the surrounding area, as this scene on Saturday 3 July 1965 shows. *(Northampton Chronicle & Echo)*

162. (below) Saturday 30 July 1960 sees the arrival at the Cattle Market of a 'right motley crew' advertising the forthcoming donkey races at Grendon Gymkhana on August Bank Holiday Monday.
(Northampton Chronicle & Echo)

163. Another view from the Plough Hotel in Bridge Street, this time looking towards the Gasworks along Weston Street on Tuesday 2 June 1959. Work has begun in earnest on the construction of St Peter's Way, and it was to take another two years before being finally completed in October 1961. On the left, part of the Phipps brewery complex can be seen, now replaced by Carlsberg. Over 35 years later one of the huge gasometers still survives, as does the building immediately below it. This used to belong to the Northampton Gas Light Company. On the horizon in the background only St Peter's Church has survived the years of modernization which followed. (*Northampton Chronicle & Echo*)

164. Another wet day on Monday 15 May 1967 and a scene photographed at the lower end of Bridge Street looking towards the town centre with the Plough Hotel prominent in the centre of the picture. The name Arthur Mulliner was synonymous with this part of the town and his firm was famous for its coachbuilding. Fine horse carriages had been made since 1760 and were built to a very high standard. Arthur Mulliner's works can be seen on the right-hand side of the picture behind the Malt Shovel public house. *(Northampton Chronicle & Echo)*

165. (facing page) South Bridge looking towards the town centre during 1913. The electric trams did not start running on this route until October 1914, hence the use of the double-decker horse-drawn omnibuses on which the fare into town was 1d. The Crown & Anchor public house was demolished during 1935. *(Northampton Borough Council Archive)*

166. (above) South Bridge looking towards town centre on Wednesday 14 October 1953. The horse-drawn buses, Crown & Anchor public house and the tall chimney have all passed into history, but very little else has changed over 40 years, even the fare into town by a modern bus was only 2½d. During the early 1970s the breweries on the left were demolished to make way for the new Carlsberg brewery. *(Northampton Chronicle & Echo)*

167/168. Another well-known landmark in Northampton was the attractive structure of the former Crown maltings, built in 1877 and standing adjacent to South Bridge. Despite having a preservation order put on it, the building was mysteriously gutted by fire during December 1977, and the inevitable demolition took place in April 1979. The view from the west side (above) of the bridge shows Cotton End Wharf and Lock No. 17 at the end of the Northampton arm of the Grand Union Canal. In the background are timber yards that were once supplied by boat from London Docks. The view from the east side (right) photographed on Saturday 1 August 1964 shows the warehouse as being owned by Lankester & Wells, whilst in the foreground one of the many swans that still frequent the River Nene makes a landing in the water.
(167. Robin Puryer
168. Northampton Chronicle & Echo)

169. A part of Northampton that is little known is the Cotton End Wharf on the canal. Here the gaunt building of black corrugated iron that is the Cotton End warehouse still stands. In this view, photographed on Monday 23 March 1964, the British Waterways warehouse was still being used as a road haulage depot and boat-building yard. A British Railways 'mechanical horse' on the left is being loaded with goods, while a clutch of barges are moored on the canal. The building was built by the Grand Junction Canal Company in 1926. November 1962 was the last time a canal-borne load was handled at the warehouse. *(Northampton Chronicle & Echo)*

170. During the 1926 General Strike the Northampton trams continued running, much to the annoyance of the strikers. Here at Cotton End it appears a confrontation is taking place, probably with the railwaymen, on the town side of Bridge Street level crossing, forcing the passengers to disembark from the trams and continue their journey on foot. *(Northampton Borough Council Archive)*

171. A nostalgic look at Cotton End by the level crossing on Saturday 29 October 1960 reveals a traffic survey in full swing causing the usual congestion. Note the wonderful collection of period motor cars as well as the entrance to Bridge Street Station and the long gone row of shops in the background. Bridge Street signalbox can just be seen on the left-hand side with the familiar footbridge over the railway at this point also noticeable. One wonders how access to the station was possible on this day with so many obstructions in the way! *(Northampton Chronicle & Echo)*

172. Traffic jams at the Bridge Street level crossing were a regular occurrence in the days when the Northampton to Peterborough line was open. Once a train was signalled it sometimes took some five to ten minutes to arrive! In this scene on Tuesday 7 October 1958 on a grim rainy day the gates have just opened after a long wait, and a huge plume of exhaust smoke is left hanging in the air by the first car through. Nowadays the amount of rail traffic has decreased dramatically and, with alternative routes, the problem has disappeared. Incredibly, the buildings in the background still existed in 1994, and even the Cotton End street name-plate remained. (*Northampton Chronicle & Echo*)

173. The familiar footbridge at Bridge Street level crossing survived until the close of Bridge Street station in 1964. For railway enthusiasts it acted as an excellent viewing location, and for the energetic and impatient cyclist it offered a means of avoiding delay when the gates were shut to traffic – many would carry their bikes up the steps and down the other side. At this time the bell hanging outside the signalbox was still used by the signalman as a warning that the gates were about to be shut.
(Northampton Chronicle & Echo)

174/175. Heavy traffic at the Cotton End/St Leonard's Road junction on Saturday 13 May 1950 as people head towards Silverstone to watch the British and European Grand Prix (given the name 'Grand Prix d'Europe'), the first round of the new post-war motor racing World Championship series. The 70-lap event was dominated by the Alfa Romeos and was watched by Their Majesties King George VI and Queen Elizabeth, and HRH Princess Margaret, who also visited the pits. On the left of the picture the old tram shelter is still being used as a bus stop. (*Northampton Chronicle & Echo*)

176. The loco shed yard at Far Cotton at lunchtime on a cold overcast Sunday 21 February 1965 – a view from which only St Mary's Church has survived the ravages of redevelopment. The watering column, kept from freezing by the two fiercely burning braziers, nicely frames the church spire, while the backs of the houses in Oxford Street merge with the single building in Main Road to complete a nostalgic railway scene. *(Robin Puryer)*

177. Far Cotton in the vicinity of the locomotive shed in 1959. On the left the Victorian terraced houses of Oxford, Rickard and Henley Streets are prominent. Main Road runs up the middle of the picture, passing the Northamptonshire Farmers building and ending at the site of Airflow Streamlines Ltd. The locomotive shed with its coaling stage and ash disposal plant can be seen on the right-hand side, and the Northampton arm of the Grand Union Canal runs parallel to the shed lines, passing first under the Blisworth line and then the Northampton to Euston line and reaching lock No. 16 near Duston West signalbox. The 15-arches viaduct carries the Euston line over the River Nene in the top right-hand corner. *(Airflow Streamlines)*

178. (above) Beyond Main Road a lone cyclist rides along the track that leads to the railway. In this glimpse a Euston to Wolverhampton express coasts downhill into Northampton behind Coronation class Pacific No. 46256 SIR WILLIAM A. STANIER F.R.S. on Sunday 10 March 1963. The pile of bricks on the left now forms part of the Rothersthorpe Road Industrial Estate. *(Graham Onley)*

179. (below) A diverted Euston to Liverpool express coasts downhill past Duston West signalbox behind Coronation Pacific No. 46243 CITY OF LANCASTER on Sunday 2 September 1962. In the background houses in Thirlestone Crescent and Rothersthorpe Road can be seen, while the field in the foreground will later form part of a housing development. *(Graham Onley)*

180. Disruption to rush hour traffic in London Road, Delapré, on the approach to Northampton on a snowy Tuesday 9 January 1968. The problem seems to be with the traffic climbing up the hill out of town, but an old Austin has apparently found sufficient grip to proceed, leaving more modern vehicles behind. Over 25 years later snowfall still results in such delays. *(Northampton Chronicle & Echo)*

181. The Queen Eleanor cross on the London Road photographed around 1880. A scene that fortunately changes very little. The cross was erected sometime between 1291 and 1294 to mark one of the resting places on Edward I's long journey to London with the coffin containing his queen, Eleanor of Castile, who had died at Harby in Nottinghamshire on 28 November 1290. The cortege arrived at Northampton on 7 December, and the body of the queen is believed to have rested the night in the convent church of St Mary-in-the-Meadow at the Delapré Cluniac Nunnery. On leaving in the morning this site was chosen and consecrated for the erection of the cross. Altogether 12 crosses were erected on the route taken, three of which remain, including this one and the cross at Geddington. *(H. Mansfield)*

HIGHWAYS AND BYWAYS
Views towards Kingsthorpe

182. (facing page) The Drapery looking north from the Lloyds Bank building in George Row during 1953. The street name is long-established, but in 1483 only the west side was known by this name; the east side being called The Glovery because of the many glovemakers occupying the premises. The buildings are of a variety of architectural styles. The branch of Westminster Bank was established here in 1928, and the renowned chemist Philadelphus Jeyes, on the left, started business in 1810 and continued until recent years. *(Northampton Chronicle & Echo)*

183. (above) On the Saturday evening of 30 September 1933 two double-decker and three single-decker trams stand forlornly parked in the Drapery after being ousted from the Kingsthorpe route by the new buses. This left the trams to work the Far Cotton and St James routes for another 14 months before their total demise. The 'Cars for Kingsthorpe' sign obviously refers to tram cars and will soon be altered to Bus Stop! *(W.J.S. Meredith)*

184. Saturday 27 November 1965 and a busy mid-morning scene in a rain-drenched Drapery. At the top of the street can just be seen the Odeon cinema. This started out in 1920 called the Exchange cinema and had a spell as the Gaumont before becoming the Odeon. It showed its final film in 1974 after which it became a Bingo hall. The familiar bus stops on the left-hand side of the street are still in existence, where people living in the north of the town have queued in times past.
(*Northampton Chronicle & Echo*)

185. A typical street scene in Sheep Street looking towards The Drapery on Tuesday 17 May 1938 with hardly any traffic. The Bag Stores building built in 1901 can still be seen today, but much of the right-hand side has been demolished. The Bear Hotel remained for many years and can be seen in picture 186. *(W.J.S. Meredith)*

186. Sheep Street (25 years later than picture 185) on Wednesday 4 December 1963, and generally the scene had not changed much. Many of the small shops on the left-hand side of the street had been in business for a long time in the town, Sigwart's being one of them. Some of the shops remain, largely towards the town side of Sheep Street, but many of the buildings on the left have been demolished for road schemes. *(Northampton Chronicle & Echo)*

187. A wander along Sheep Street brings one down to the Regent Square area of Northampton. This view, photographed on Wednesday 4 December 1963, looks towards the town centre and is overlooked by the spire of St Sepulchre's Church. More road widening schemes in recent years have meant the demolition of the first three buildings on the left of the picture, but fortunately the rest remain to show the varied architecture. On the right-hand side of the street the public lavatories have gone along with most of the buildings in this area. *(Northampton Chronicle & Echo)*

188. (above) The well-known 101 Club photographed in March 1971 can still be seen on the corner of Sheep Street and Broad Street under new management but still as a club. A nostalgic look down Broad Street towards Mayor Hold shows a street of many fine buildings, all to be demolished soon after to make way for yet another road improvement scheme. *(Northampton Borough Council)*

189. (below) At the bottom of Broad Street the well-known landmark of Nicholson's wool factory in the Mayor Hold can be seen on Tuesday 7 November 1967. Bull Head Lane, at the corner of the building, leads off towards Sheep Street. This area was to disappear without trace during the redevelopment of the 1970s. *(Northampton Borough Council)*

190. It is Friday 9 July 1965 in Mayor Hold, with Nicholson's factory in the background, and the clutter of Northampton Transport buses (nearly all Daimlers) results from a diversion from the town centre because today is the day Her Majesty the Queen is visiting Northampton. Mayor Hold was always a busy part of the town as many bus companies used it as a terminus. *(Robin Puryer)*

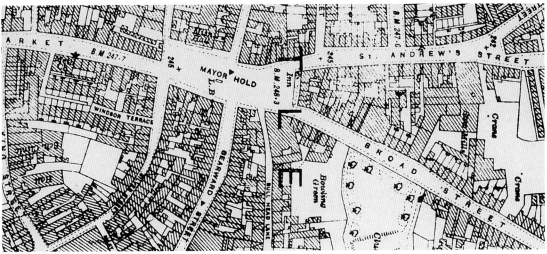

191. This scene, from one of the multi-storey blocks of flats erected in the old 'Boroughs' area of Northampton in 1963, photographed in March 1971, shows the Mayor Hold undergoing major redevelopment. At this time it was still possible to see, from left to right, Bull Head Lane, Bearward Street and Silver Street leading off the Mayor Hold and running up towards the town centre. Many Northamptonians of the 50s and 60s will remember the shops in Mayor Hold – Bottrill the confectioner, Pitt the butcher and, sandwiched in between, one of the many Co-operative buildings that could be found in the town. This was Branch No. 11 and was built in 1919. Nowadays this view would be unrecognizable as the area has been totally redeveloped. On the horizon to the right of the tower of the Guildhall can be seen one of the cooling towers of the Power Station. (*Northampton Borough Council*)

192. Taken from Northampton's first high rise block, St Katherine's Court, in August 1957 just prior to its completion, this picture looks south-east towards the town centre, and many familiar landmarks can be seen on the horizon. From left to right: the Guildhall, All Saints Church and the Power Station. In the foreground Horsemarket is visible beyond the car park and St Katherine Street starts at the corner where the café is. At the time Grose's Garage was in Marefair and three of the company's vehicles can be seen parked on waste-ground near the garage. In years to come many of the buildings in the foreground, this side of the trees, were demolished, but beyond the trees much of the town area was to survive. *(W.J.S. Meredith)*

193. From January 1963 there was another high level viewpoint with the completion of two more multi-storey blocks of flats. This picture, however, was taken on 11 September 1961 during construction. The view is north-north-east and shows much of the Victorian terraced housing in the Semilong area of Northampton. St Andrew's Church was sadly demolished during August 1972, together with the houses in the surrounding area, to make way for a new carriageway. In the background, behind St Andrew's, stands Marlow's shoe factory in St George's Street, with its elaborate corner tower, built in 1890. It was known as the Phoenix Boots Works. In the foreground terraced houses in Cooper Street running off Bell Barn Street, and to the left Harding Street, show what was still left of the 'Boroughs' area of the town. (*Northampton Chronicle & Echo*)

194. A rare view along St Andrew's Street in the summer of 1938 looking towards St Andrew's Church. On the left Bell Barn Street leads on to Grafton Square, while to the right St Andrew's Street continues to Grafton Street. On the corner of the street junction Mr Masters's grocery store can be seen, and on the left some excellent examples of the cars of the period are parked. The only building that is still in existence is the one with the whitewashed frontage on the far right of the picture standing in Grafton Street. *(W.J.S. Meredith)*

195/196/197. The busy Regent Square junction has changed over the years, and here are three views from different angles. Picture 195 (above), photographed in 1937, shows the driver of a 1930 'juggernaut' relaxing in between duties, while demolition of the old laundry building continues. No doubt, even in those days, the Express Transport Service company based in Wellingborough was in competition with the Leicester & County Carriers. In the background are residential properties situated in Barrack Road. Picture 196 (top right), photographed in October 1954, shows an elevated view of the Square. Alas The Bull Hotel is no more, having been demolished, along with the whitewashed building opposite, in another road widening scheme, but at least the brick-built terraced homes in Campbell Street have survived. Picture 197 (bottom right) viewed from Campbell Street and looking towards Grafton Street on the left and St George's Street on the right, was also photographed in October 1954. It shows the building from which picture 196 was taken. Many of these buildings remain in use, although most of the small businesses have either changed hands or stopped trading altogether. Parsonson's is a long-established Northampton firm.

(195. W.J.S. Meredith)

(196/197. Northampton Chronicle & Echo)

196.

197.

198. (left) This deserted scene, showing St George's Place, was photographed from the roof of the Roman Catholic church on 9 March 1964. The Barratt shoe factory (built in 1913) is on the far left of the picture, and two more modern shoe factories can also be seen in the background in Freehold Street. The terraced homes of Balfour Road and Balmoral Road lie beyond these with the Holy Trinity Church almost at the top left of the picture. The multi-storey block of Trinity School can be seen on the horizon to the right of the picture. Nowadays, not only are many cars always parked on both sides of the road, but traffic seems continuous.
(*Northampton Chronicle & Echo*)

199. (below) A tram car clatters up the hill from Kingsthorpe Hollow towards the town centre on Monday 18 September 1933, just nine days before the trams ceased running on this route. The photographer has captured an extremely rare picture with this view on top of the tram car which on this day is surprisingly empty. On the right the houses in St George's Place lead down to the Barratt shoe factory. (*W.J.S. Meredith*)

200. This winter view looking at Kingsthorpe Hollow towards the town centre was photographed during 1953. A solitary lorry plods its way up the hill on an otherwise nigh-empty road – a distinct contrast to the many vehicles that use the road today. To the left, Balmoral Road can be seen, and on the right is one of Grose's service garages, with others being advertised in grand manner on the side of one of the buildings. One wonders how long it took to signwrite all that information!
(Northampton Chronicle & Echo)

201. How many Northamptonians can remember Mill Lane in Kingsthorpe? This wintry scene was photographed on Monday 13 January 1964 after an overnight fall of snow. A Vauxhall Cresta carefully negotiates the bends as it heads towards Kings Heath. In the background is Kingsthorpe Church. How different from a modern day Mill Lane scene! *(Northampton Chronicle & Echo)*

INDEX

202. A tram stands at the St James terminus in Weedon Road opposite the junction with Glasgow Street during 1934, the last year of operation. The building on the right was part of Franklin's Gardens, a popular park and entertainment centre covering some 30 acres at its zenith. *(W.J.S. Meredith)*